Please mail to: Foreign Policy Association, 205 Lexington Avenue,
New York, NY 10016, or call (212) 481-8450

Please enter my subscription to FPA's bimonthly *Headline Series*—lively and provocative publications (usually 64 pages) on current problems and critical areas of the world. (Five issues per year—January, March, May, September and November.)

☐ $12 for one year ☐ $20 for two years ☐ $28 for three years

(Please add $1.50 *per year* for postage outside the U.S.; $6.00 *per year* for first class mail outside the U.S.)

Please send me the following latest issues in the *Headline Series:*

_____ copies of HS 270, *Arms Control—Verification and Compliance,* by Michael Krepon

_____ copies of HS 269, *The Two Koreas* by Bruce Cumings

_____ copies of HS 268, *The Atlantic Alliance at 35* by A.W. DePorte

_____ copies of HS 267, *Mexico: Neighbor in Transition* by Peter H. Smith

_____ copies of HS 266, *The Puerto Rican Question* by Jorge Heine and Juan M. García-Passalacqua

_____ copies of HS 265, *The U.S.S.R. After Brezhnev* by Seweryn Bialer

_____ copies of HS 264, *Human Rights and the Helsinki Accord* by William Korey

_____ copies of HS 263, *Vietnam: The War Nobody Won* by Stanley Karnow

_____ copies of HS 262, *India in the 1980s* by Phillips Talbot

_____ copies of HS 261, *Nuclear Strategy and Arms Control* by Stanley R. Sloan and Robert C. Gray

Price: $3.00 each

Discounts available for ten or more copies.
Write or call for discount information.

(see reverse side)

FPA INFORMATION/ORDER FORM

Please mail to: Foreign Policy Association, 205 Lexington Avenue, New York, NY 10016, or call (212) 481-8450

Please send me:

_____ copies of **Foreign Policy Choices for Americans**
by the editors of the Foreign Policy Association
Price: $5.95 each

_____ copies of **Great Decisions '85,** FPA's 96-page, news-magazine-size publication with impartial background and analysis of eight critical foreign policy issues facing the U.S.
Price: Paperback—$6.00   Hardcover—$15.00

☐ a free copy of FPA's latest catalogue of publications

☐ a free copy of FPA's latest annual report

Send to: (please print)

Name _____

Address _____

City _____ State _____ Zip _____

Payment must accompany orders. Please include $1.00 for postage and handling. Checks should be made payable to Foreign Policy Association.

Discounts available for ten or more copies.
Write or call for discount information.

(see reverse side)

Headline Series

No. 270   FOREIGN POLICY ASSOCIATION $3.00

ARMS CONTROL
VERIFICATION AND COMPLIANCE
by Michael Krepon

Introduction   3

1
Basic Concepts of Verification   5

2
The Politics of Verification   14

3
Soviet Views on Verification   28

4
Treaty Compliance   35

5
Compliance Diplomacy   46

Glossary   61
Talking It Over   63
Annotated Reading List   64

Cover by Hersch Wartik;
adapted from design by Cathy Canzani

September/October 1984

The Author

MICHAEL KREPON is a Senior Associate at the Carnegie Endowment for International Peace, where he directs the verification project. The project is supported by a grant from the Ploughshares Fund. He served in the Carter Administration, directing defense project and policy reviews at the Arms Control and Disarmament Agency. He previously worked on Capitol Hill as assistant to Congressman Norman D. Dicks (D-Wash.). He is the author of *Strategic Stalemate, Nuclear Weapons and Arms Control in American Politics*, to be published in the fall of 1984 by St. Martin's Press.

The Foreign Policy Association

The Foreign Policy Association is a private, nonprofit, nonpartisan educational organization. Its purpose is to stimulate wider interest and more effective participation in, and greater understanding of, world affairs among American citizens. Among its activities is the continuous publication, dating from 1935, of the HEADLINE SERIES. The author is responsible for factual accuracy and for the views expressed. FPA itself takes no position on issues of U.S. foreign policy.

Editorial Advisory Committee
Chairman: Stanley H. Hoffmann

Members
Carol Edler Baumann
Earl W. Foell
John Lewis Gaddis
Edwin Newman
Ponchitta Pierce

Eleanor Singer
Andrew F. Smith
James A. Van Fleet
Samuel S. Vaughan
Leo M. Weins
Allen Weinstein

HEADLINE SERIES (ISSN 0017-8780) is published five times a year, January, March, May, September and November, by the Foreign Policy Association, Inc., 205 Lexington Ave., New York, N.Y. 10016. Chairman, Leonard H. Marks; President, Archie E. Albright; Editor, Nancy L. Hoepli; Associate Editors, Ann R. Monjo and Mary E. Stavrou. Subscription rates, $12.00 for 5 issues; $20.00 for 10 issues; $28.00 for 15 issues. Single copy price $3.00. Discount 25% on 10 to 99 copies; 30% on 100 to 499; 35% on 500 to 999; 40% on 1,000 or more. Payment must accompany order for $6 or less. Second-class postage paid at New York, N.Y. POSTMASTER: Send address changes to HEADLINE SERIES, Foreign Policy Association, 205 Lexington Ave., New York, N.Y. 10016. Copyright 1984 by Foreign Policy Association, Inc. Composed and printed at Science Press, Ephrata, Pa.

Library of Congress Catalog No. 84-82069
ISBN 0-87124-093-9

Introduction

The importance of verifying compliance with arms control agreements is self-evident: the United States should be able to know whether negotiated agreements are being observed. The premise is simple, but the topics of verification and compliance are complex. National security experts argue about the "verifiability" of various provisions within arms control agreements and about the record of Soviet compliance. Their debates are frequently waged in language foreign to most American citizens.

This HEADLINE SERIES issue is geared to a nonexpert audience that wants to know more about verification and compliance. One does not need to be conversant with new developments in verification technology or the details of classified information to reach informed judgments. If concerned citizens take the time to familiarize themselves with the issues discussed in these pages, they can become informed participants in public debates, despite their complexities.

This book was written under the auspices of the Carnegie Endowment for International Peace, where the author is a Senior Associate in charge of the verification project. The project is supported by a grant from the Ploughshares Fund, whose staff conceived the study. Ploughshares and the Foreign Policy Association have agreed to extend the press run of this HEADLINE SERIES issue to facilitate its distribution to citizens interested in national security issues. The verification project was initiated at the Roosevelt Center for American Policy Studies in Washington, D.C.

A number of experts with backgrounds in arms control negotiations, congressional affairs, intelligence, diplomacy, defense, science and reporting agreed to advise and critique materials written for the verification project. Project advisers include William Beecher, Barry Blechman, Robert Buchheim, Lt. Gen. Kelly Burke (USAF, Ret.), Frank Church, William Colby, Sidney Drell, Ralph Earle II, Alton Frye, Mark Garrison, Leslie Gelb, Sidney Graybeal, Arnold Horelick, Thomas L. Hughes, Frank Jenkins, Spurgeon Keeny, Ray McCrory, Roger Molander, William Perry, George Schneiter, Lt. Gen. George Seignious II (USA, Ret.), Walter Slocombe, Gerard Smith, Howard Stoertz, Strobe Talbott, Lt. Gen. Eugene Tighe (USAF, Ret.), Adm. Stansfield Turner (USN, Ret.), and Paul Warnke. These advisers graciously offered the author the benefit of their considerable insight and expertise. Their names are listed here to acknowledge their help, not to suggest their endorsement of the views expressed in the pages that follow. I also wish to thank Gloria Duffy and Sara Goodgame without whose assistance this book could not have been written. Portions have been drawn from papers delivered at conferences at the University of California at Los Angeles and the Massachusetts Institute of Technology, and from an article in the fall 1984 issue of *Foreign Policy*.

1

Basic Concepts of Verification

With or without arms control agreements, the United States must collect and assess information concerning Soviet military capabilities. The U.S.S.R. has formidable land, sea and air power that can be projected far afield against U.S. friends and allies. Soviet nuclear capabilities can be directed with catastrophic effects against American targets in a matter of minutes. These capabilities, both nuclear and conventional, do not remain static. The size of weapon inventories changes; some older weapon systems are retired while more-capable systems take their place. Changes occur in military organizations, in training practices and in the patterns of military operations that provide clues concerning Soviet military capabilities and intentions.

U.S. political and military officials need to know as much as they can about Soviet military power in order to protect the nation's security. Arms control agreements can also promote American security by placing limits on Soviet forces and by contributing to more-predictable and stable relations with the Soviet Union. Negotiated agreements can prevent an open-ended competition that increases the likelihood of a military confrontation that neither side wants and a nuclear war that neither side can win. But the United States cannot trust the Soviet Union to adhere to these agreements; the United States must be able to verify Soviet compliance.

Arms control limits are monitored by the same methods we use to observe Soviet military power. Specific provisions in arms control agreements may add somewhat to these monitoring tasks, or may require that U.S. monitoring capabilities be applied to answer very specific questions.

Debates about verification center around basic assumptions concerning the value of arms control, Soviet objectives and the risks of Soviet cheating. Those who are inclined to believe that arms control agreements are of limited value and that the Kremlin's hostile objectives and proclivity to cheat are immutable require very stringent verification standards for any agreement. Those who believe that arms control agreements can be of mutual benefit and that the Soviets will see the wisdom of refraining from cheating—especially cheating that is of little or no military significance—will find more-flexible verification requirements acceptable.

Compliance with complex arms control agreements cannot be verified with absolute confidence. Sometimes the provisions to be monitored are vague, either because both sides are unable or do not wish to be more precise. And even the most sophisticated monitoring devices may not clarify ambiguous events. As a result, there will always be risks involved in monitoring arms control agreements. The problem for policymakers is to determine how much risk is acceptable.

The intelligence community assigns "confidence levels" reflecting its judgment of the U.S. ability to detect prohibited activity. A "high" confidence level indicates between a 90 and 100 percent assurance of detecting a prohibited activity—or a zero to 10 percent risk that we will be uncertain about whether our treaty partner is in compliance; a "moderate" confidence level corresponds to a 50 to 75 percent chance of detection; a "low" confidence level indicates a 10 to 50 percent chance of detection.

The SALT I* (strategic arms limitation talks) interim agreement* of 1972 set limits on land-based intercontinental ballistic

---

*Terms in text followed by an asterisk are defined in glossary on pages 61 and 62.

missile (ICBM) launchers and submarine-launched ballistic missile (SLBM) launchers. Both could be monitored with high confidence. The excavation of silos to launch ICBMs requires considerable time and heavy equipment, as does the movement and deployment of ICBMs into them. Likewise, SLBM launchers are contained in large submarines especially built over many years for this purpose. The deployment of SLBMs and their launchers can be monitored carefully. Thus, ever since the advent of overhead photography, the intelligence community has been forewarned of the deployment of new Soviet ICBMs, SLBMs and their launchers.

Even in the seemingly simple case of SALT I, however, judgments differed as to the adequacy of U.S. intelligence capabilities and the wisdom of arms control agreements limiting ICBM and SLBM launchers. Critics of the agreement argued that missiles as well as their launchers should be controlled because the missiles did not necessarily have to be launched from underground silos or submarines. Moreover, silos might be reused to launch additional missiles. Since the United States did not know the size of Soviet missile inventories, critics argued that the limitations imposed by the SALT I interim agreement were artificial and unsatisfactory.

In response to this critique, supporters of the agreement argued that it was not necessary to determine precisely the size of Soviet ICBM inventories, since the Soviets did not have facilities for and did not practice launching ICBMs except by means of underground silos. Supporters of SALT I also downplayed the military significance of excess missiles, given the amount of destruction that might be anticipated in the event of widespread nuclear detonations. Moreover, before the Soviets could launch ICBMs outside their missile silos, they would have to train to master this technique; and these activities could be monitored by U.S. intelligence analysts in time to prepare appropriate responses. Subsequent debates over verification have been quite similar; critics generally contend that agreements are not adequately broad in scope and that sufficiently broad agreements are not verifiable. Supporters argue that limited agreements are worth achieving, and should not be held hostage to more ambitious and perhaps unrealizable objectives.

Assessments of risk are at the core of debates over verification. Some limitations may be worthwhile but difficult to monitor. Others may be monitored with high confidence, but their impact may be slight. Take, for example, limitations on throw-weight,* or the payload* of nuclear warheads and other equipment missiles can carry. Let us assume the United States could monitor a 25 percent increase in throw-weight from one generation of missiles to the next with high confidence, but that an increase in throw-weight of 5 percent can be monitored only with moderate confidence. Let us also assume that an increase in throw-weight of 25 percent could result in a substantial increase in military capabilities, whereas an increase in throw-weight of 5 percent would provide only a marginal difference. Should public officials opt for a 5 percent limitation which would be difficult to monitor, or a 25 percent limitation which would be relatively easy to monitor? On the one hand, there is a greater risk in monitoring a 5 percent limitation. On the other hand, there is a greater military risk in choosing a 25 percent limitation.

National Technical Means

Intelligence analysts and political leaders rely on sophisticated technical devices to monitor Soviet military activities. When used to monitor compliance with arms control agreements, these devices are collectively known as national technical means* of verification.

Among the many types of national technical means, photoreconnaissance satellites* are best known, perhaps because of pictures released during the Cuban missile crisis of October 1962 which clearly depicted the construction of Soviet missile sites on the island. Two decades later, President Ronald Reagan released photographs of military construction in Nicaragua to support his contention of widespread Soviet and Cuban support for the

Nicaraguan government. In both cases, these pictures were actually taken by reconnaissance aircraft rather than satellites. The United States has not released publicly military satellite photographs on the grounds that to do so would lead to other disclosures and reveal too much information about U.S. overhead reconnaissance capabilities. The very existence of these satellites was not acknowledged officially until 1978.

Perhaps because of the secrecy associated with U.S. picture-taking satellites, extraordinary claims have been made on their behalf, such as their ability to read numbers on license plates or see through buildings. Photoreconnaissance satellites can do extraordinary things, but they are not capable of these magical feats. The photoreconnaissance satellites' capability to distinguish objects varies depending on their specifications and mission—whether to provide wide-area surveillance or a close look at a specific object of interest. Any government official who has seen pictures taken from space can attest to their clarity. According to one former director of the Central Intelligence Agency (CIA), they can allow skilled photo-interpreters to distinguish between Guernseys and Herefords grazing in a meadow. However, satellite coverage is not always available when needed. Because of their high cost, very few picture-taking satellites are in orbit at any one time. Those orbits traverse different sections of the Soviet Union approximately once every 90 minutes.

Standard photographic techniques cannot penetrate cloud cover and are of no use during nighttime, but there are other ways to take pictures from space. Advances in radar imagery, where pictures are produced by bouncing radio waves against a field of view, are particularly important since radar can operate day and night, irrespective of cloud cover. Pictures can also be derived from the heat emitted from objects by means of thermal infrared scanners. Another useful technique is multispectral photography, where separate lenses shoot simultaneous pictures in different regions of the electromagnetic spectrum. This technique allows photo-interpreters to distinguish between true vegetation and camouflage which would not be apparent otherwise.

Engineers in the Soviet Union, like those in the United States, test new weapon systems extensively to have confidence that they will work as designed. Operators of this equipment also want to test it repeatedly to train their forces and to check on its reliability. These test programs usually take place over several years at specific, usually well-known, locations. From past practices, for example, U.S. intelligence analysts have come to associate launches of new missile types with one of four test locations in the Soviet Union. Missile flight tests are both inescapable and very informative.

Imagine the test launch of a new Soviet ICBM. Almost immediately, U.S. satellites with infrared sensors detect the heat of the missile's exhaust, providing early warning to American officials of the launch. (In most cases, this information only confirms previous indications of an expected launch, as U.S. analysts usually pick up preparatory signs of the test, again through national technical means.) The early-warning satellites are 22,000 miles up in geosynchronous* orbits which allow them to monitor Soviet territory continuously. After the launch, U.S. ground stations on the periphery of the Soviet Union track the missile's progress and, when possible, monitor the radio messages or telemetry* transmitted to Soviet engineers.

Airborne, sea-, and ground-based radars monitor the progress and conclusion of missile flight tests. The reentry points for long-range Soviet missile tests are in the Kamchatka peninsula in the Soviet Far East, or in the Pacific Ocean. The United States has built a large, "phased-array"* radar in the Aleutian Islands, 450 miles from Kamchatka. This radar, designated Cobra Dane, can monitor electronically Soviet warheads 2,000 miles from their impact point, continuing to track their descent through the atmosphere. Another phased array located aboard a specially equipped ship, Cobra Judy, also may be used for this purpose.

During an earlier era, Secretary of State Henry M. Stimson (1929–33) objected to U.S. code-breaking operations on the basis that "Gentlemen don't read each other's mail." Today, eavesdropping on military communications is a standard practice and a central component of intelligence collection. "Ferret" satellites and aircraft specialize in electromagnetic reconnaissance, keyed to Soviet radar emissions and patterns of communications. The information gathered by monitoring Soviet communications helps to provide a composite picture of military programs, operations and strategy.

In 1963, the United States launched the first in a series of satellites to detect tests of nuclear weapons in the atmosphere. These satellites have been deployed in pairs at extremely high orbits so as to provide nearly worldwide coverage at all times. To monitor nuclear weapon tests underground, the United States relies on a worldwide system of seismic stations that record the energy generated by underground explosions. For many years, experts have disputed the ability of this network of seismic stations to distinguish between tests of nuclear weapons at very low yields and earthquakes. Another point of contention has been the utility and likelihood of muffling underground nuclear weapon tests (a process known as "decoupling") to evade detection.

Cooperative Measures

While the diversity and capability of national technical means of verification are impressive, they are often insufficient to monitor military capabilities that parties may wish to include in arms control agreements. For example, no matter how good the picture-taking ability of a photoreconnaissance satellite, it cannot determine how many warheads are placed atop a missile located within a silo.

The United States and the Soviet Union agreed to a bookkeeping solution to the problem of counting warheads: "counting rules"* were developed in the SALT II* treaty, signed by President Jimmy Carter and General Secretary Leonid I. Brezhnev in 1979, that allowed both sides to count deployed warheads by assigning a specified number of warheads to each type of missile. The Reagan Administration has given this approach increasing prominence in the strategic arms reduction talks (START)* that began in June 1982 but were suspended in December 1983. Counting rules are possible for warheads because U.S. and Soviet intelligence analysts can monitor the number of warheads actually released during missile flight tests. The mechanism making these releases is known as a "bus"; it carries multiple independently targetable reentry vehicles, or MIRVs,* dropping each one off at a precise point of the missile's trajectory.

Debates continue over what counting rules are most appropriate for specific agreements, but most observers believe that the risks associated with this technique are marginal while the benefits are substantial. Counting rules demonstrate how cooperative measures developed in arms control negotiations can make verification easier.

In the past, discussions of verification capabilities and requirements have often been confined to extremely narrow topics: How small an object can be spotted from space? Or, how well can this or that clause within an arms control agreement be monitored? While an ability to monitor a specific provision within an arms control agreement may be extremely important, a narrow focus can skew calculations of overall benefits and risks, including the broad risk of forfeiting a useful agreement by leaving out difficult-to-monitor weapons or by demanding unacceptably intrusive monitoring rights. All too often, narrow debates obscure the true strengths of U.S. verification capabilities; the United States relies on many different and complementary means of intelligence to provide it with a composite picture of Soviet military activities. As a result of these capabilities, the United States has detailed knowledge of current and prospective Soviet military developments. The last time the United States was surprised by a new Soviet program with strategic significance was when Sputnik, the U.S.S.R.'s first satellite, was launched in 1957, prior to the advent of photoreconnaissance satellites. The information garnered by national technical means has allowed American Presidents to assess Soviet military power, to structure U.S. forces accordingly, and to sign arms control agreements with the Kremlin.

In the future, debates over verification will be more intense because new weapons like cruise missiles are being produced that are more difficult to monitor than forces included in previous agreements. Cruise missiles are highly accurate, pilotless aircraft that can be launched from air, land or sea. They can carry conventional or nuclear weapons, and can fly short or long distances. The United States and the Soviet Union are also placing greater reliance on mobile missiles instead of missiles housed in underground silos. These developments are prompted by both sides' wish to take advantage of new technological developments and their increasing concern about the survivability of their nuclear forces. As a result, each side is diversifying the platforms that can be used to launch nuclear forces and placing a premium on mobility to foil a surprise attack. At the same time, both superpowers are emphasizing accuracy in their new weapons, as each believes highly accurate forces will best deter the other and provide advantages in the event of war. The trend toward more accurate forces reinforces the trend of exploiting new technologies and making weapons less vulnerable.

As a result of these developments, political leaders and concerned citizens will be required to make difficult choices in the future: the United States can either choose to include or exclude these hard-to-verify weapons within the scope of future agreements. Including these forces will entail greater risks in verification, but excluding them will result in less meaningful agreements.

2
The Politics of Verification

In public and congressional debates over verification, familiar arguments are offered by those at opposite ends of the political spectrum. People most concerned about the dangers of the nuclear arms race are not particularly worried about verification. Those who favor arms control but are also concerned about Soviet behavior weigh the risks of verification against the potential benefits of agreements. Those most skeptical of Soviet intentions usually see little benefit in arms control agreements and call for very stringent standards of verification.

Supporters of previous treaties argued that monitoring standards should not be so exacting as to foreclose agreement, since arms control can improve U.S. security by placing limits on Soviet forces and stabilizing the most dangerous element of the competition between the superpowers. Instead, monitoring standards should be adequate to detect Soviet cheating of military consequence, and to detect it in time to take appropriate action. In this view, the Soviets may try to cheat, but if they do, they run the risk of getting caught and jeopardizing the benefits that led them to sign an agreement. As General Secretary Brezhnev told President Richard M. Nixon at the 1972 Moscow summit, "If we are trying to trick one another, why do we need a piece of paper?" Arms controllers also argue that U.S. detection capabilities provide a deterrent to Soviet cheating, since detection would, at the very least, be embarrassing politically and could prompt a reaction that would hurt the cheater.

Those skeptical of previous agreements take a very different view of their benefits and risks. For them, agreements do not alter long-term Soviet goals, but they can hinder U.S. defense programs necessary to foil those goals. According to this view of arms control, there are few incentives—bureaucratic or otherwise—for Soviet compliance with negotiated agreements. To the contrary, the Kremlin can be expected to cheat on agreements that constrain military forces they consider necessary to achieve national objectives. The Kremlin's bureaucracy is less interested in preserving agreements than in gaining advantage—particularly when their activities do not jeopardize the agreements because of a weak U.S. response.

For those most suspicious of Soviet intentions, U.S. failure to detect cheating is no guarantee that the Kremlin is behaving itself; it means only that violations have gone undetected because of the effectiveness of the Soviet arts of deception and concealment. Since, by definition, the United States will never find anything the Soviets have successfully hidden, the possibilities of cheating—and the resulting harm to U.S. security—are endless. It follows that the only acceptable arms control agreement is one that sets strict standards for verification, contains highly intrusive monitoring provisions and a forceful policy of sanctions, and permits unilateral actions once a violation is detected.

Most Americans and their elected officials do not take dogmatic stands on verification issues. There is a wide variety of views on the value of negotiated agreements and appropriate standards of verification. Competing political slogans about "never trusting the Russians" or "trusting the Russians to act in their own best interests" provide little help for the toughest judgment calls over verification and risk. But particularly of late, the terms of political debate have been set by those at opposite ends of the political spectrum.

'Adequate' Verification, 1963-79

For nuclear arms control agreements negotiated between 1963 and 1979, American Presidents explicitly supported a flexible approach to verification requirements. The first such agreement was the limited test ban treaty* of 1963, which barred nuclear weapon tests in the atmosphere, outer space and underwater. Officials in the Kennedy Administration agreed with those who contended that monitoring capabilities for a limited test ban could not detect all instances of Soviet noncompliance; they maintained, however, that these were risks worth taking in the light of the perceived benefits of an agreement. As President John F. Kennedy said in his transmittal message to the Senate:

> The risks in clandestine violations under this treaty are far smaller than the risks in unlimited testing... No nation tempted to violate the treaty can be certain that an attempted violation will go undetected, given the many means of detecting nuclear explosions. The risks of detection outweigh the potential gains from violation, and the risk to the United States from such violation is outweighed by the risk of a continued unlimited nuclear arms race.

The chairman of the Joint Chiefs of Staff at that time, General Maxwell D. Taylor, also acknowledged the possibilities of clandestine Soviet testing. As a result the Joint Chiefs and some members of Congress pressed for "safeguards" along with ratification.

Those safeguards included an extensive underground nuclear test program, improved monitoring capabilities, and preparations to resume atmospheric tests in the event of Soviet noncompliance. In sum, the limited test ban treaty was defended and accepted on the basis that U.S. monitoring capabilities, though deficient in certain respects, were adequate when viewed in conjunction with other political and military factors.

At the outset of the SALT negotiations, President Nixon explicitly restated the requirement for *adequate* verification in his instructions to the SALT I negotiating team:

No arms limitation agreement can ever be absolutely verifiable. The relevant test is not an abstract ideal, but the practical standard of whether we can determine compliance adequately to safeguard our security—that is, whether we can identify attempted evasion if it occurs on a large enough scale to pose a significant risk, and whether we can do so in time to mount a sufficient response. Meeting this test is what I mean by the term 'adequate verification.'

In defending the SALT I accords, Secretary of Defense Melvin R. Laird flatly stated, "We have adequate means of verification." Little debate followed on Secretary Laird's conclusion, either in committee hearings or on the floor of Congress. Most agreed with Senator Jacob K. Javits (R-N.Y.) who stated at the conclusion of the desultory ratification debate over the antiballistic missile (ABM)* treaty in August 1972:

I do not base my approval of the treaty and the agreements upon 'trust' in the benign motives of the Soviet Union. No one is asked to do that. What I do base it on is Dr. Kissinger's assurance that there is every likelihood that the agreements will be complied with because it is in the interests of the U.S.S.R. to do so.

Verification issues were of far greater concern during the SALT II hearings because the SALT II treaty included limits on qualitative missile improvements that were more difficult to monitor than the SALT I numerical limitations, and because of the compliance issues that arose from the SALT I accords. The Carter Administration's defense of the "verifiability" of the SALT II treaty was similar to that of the Kennedy and Nixon Administrations before it. In a State Department report on the treaty, the Carter Administration presented its case in the following terms:

The anticipated SALT II agreement is adequately verifiable. This judgment is based on assessment of the verifiability of the individual provisions of the agreement and the agreement as a whole. Although the possibility of some undetected cheating in certain areas exists, such cheating would not alter the strategic balance in view of U.S. programs. Any cheating on a scale large enough to alter the strategic balance would be discovered in time to make an appropriate response. There will be areas of uncertainty, but they are not such as to permit the Soviets to produce a significant unanticipated threat to U.S. interests and those uncertainties can, in any event, be compensated for with the flexibility inherent in our own programs.

During hearings on the SALT II treaty, senior Administration officials subscribed to these precepts, but public assurances, including those of the CIA director and the chairman of the Joint Chiefs of Staff, did not alleviate congressional or public concerns. Unlike the SALT I debate, treaty opponents repeatedly pointed to numerous Soviet practices that could not be monitored easily. Events during the congressional review process, particularly the loss of Iranian monitoring stations after the fall of the shah in 1979 and the "discovery" of a Soviet military brigade in Cuba in 1980, heightened sensitivities over treaty verification. These specific incidents reinforced perceptions of presidential weakness, Soviet adventurousness, and disturbing trends in superpower fortunes and military capabilities.

'Effective' Verification, 1981–

Opponents of previous arms control agreements, including many in the Reagan Administration, had long felt that adequate verification was not sufficient. Moreover, these critics believed that previous agreements had been poorly crafted, allowing the Soviets to exploit ambiguities in treaty provisions in ways that were injurious to U.S. national security and the strategic balance. In this view, tougher verification provisions and more-exacting standards for determining adequacy were necessary for future agreements.

The new watchword proposed by Reagan Administration officials was *effective* as opposed to adequate verification, although the difference has never been spelled out. Presumably, effective verification measures will vary from one agreement to the next, but whether such provisions can be negotiated remains to be seen. U.S. "verification annexes" were in the process of preparation for both the START and the intermediate-range nuclear forces (INF)* negotiations, which opened in Geneva in November 1981, but the annexes had not been completed when the talks came to a standstill in late fall 1983. In addition, no public attempt has been made by Reagan Administration officials to define what additional monitoring provisions they deem necessary for a comprehensive test ban treaty. Administration officials have based their opposition to resuming the test ban negotiation, suspended in 1980, on the need for continued nuclear weapon tests, as well as on difficulties in verification. Resistance within the Reagan Administration to limitations on antisatellite* weapons is likewise based on verification concerns as well as on military requirements to place Soviet satellites at risk.

A complete ban on space warfare capabilities is unlikely since any missile that can be lofted into space could be used as an antisatellite weapon. The crux of the debate is over the verifiability and utility of an agreement banning antisatellite weapon tests. Reagan Administration officials argue that such tests could be concealed, particularly tests conducted by ground-based lasers. In a report to the Congress on antisatellite arms control dated March 31, 1984, the Reagan Administration concluded,

> The fact that antisatellite capabilities are inherent in some systems developed for other missions or are amenable to undetected or surreptitious development makes it impossible to verify compliance with a truly comprehensive testing limitation that would eliminate tests of all methods of countering satellites.

Given their premises that a one-sided antisatellite capability could alter the strategic balance in unacceptable ways and that some antisatellite capabilities could be tested covertly, it follows that Reagan Administration officials would prefer more-modest agreements allowing both sides some antisatellite capabilities, or no agreements at all.

Supporters of an antisatellite test ban concede a degree of risk but contend that the benefits of reaching agreement far outweigh the risks. Moreover they argue that antisatellite flight tests cannot be concealed from U.S. national technical means for very long or very well. While laser antisatellite tests might pose a problem, new national technical means could be developed to monitor them. More-conventional antisatellite tests seem far easier to recognize. Arguments to the contrary are reminiscent of earlier debates over the advisability of an agreement banning MIRVs during the Nixon Administration. At that time, some Administration officials were worried that the Soviets could disguise MIRV tests. Those fears now appear vastly overdrawn.

'Intrusive' Verification and On-Site Inspections

The most difficult arms control choices facing U.S. policymakers and elected officials relate to the scope of new agreements and the standards deemed necessary to monitor compliance. The range and consequences of these choices can be demonstrated by reviewing three case studies: the limited test ban treaty, the biological weapons convention, and the decision to link the inclusion of MIRVs in the SALT I accords to a requirement for on-site inspections.

In 1963, President Kennedy decided to conclude a limited agreement with the Soviet Union barring all nuclear weapon tests except those underground, instead of a comprehensive agreement banning all tests. Several reasons lay behind this choice, but all were tied to difficulties in monitoring a total ban and in obtaining Soviet agreement to intrusive measures needed to verify the absence of underground tests of nuclear weapons.

The most intrusive measure of verification to monitor treaty compliance is on-site inspections—whereby one treaty signatory allows a team of experts to inspect specific areas, installations or other facilities under agreed procedures. In the above-mentioned case, the United States and the Soviet Union at one point proposed respectively seven and three on-site inspections to monitor a comprehensive ban, but both sides were far apart on critical details of these inspections: how many inspectors would be permitted, the length of their stay, how much Soviet and U.S. territory they would be able to roam, and what transportation and inspection methods would be allowed.

Neither side made any great effort to narrow the distance between their positions on these operational questions, since neither could bridge the gap in the number of inspections to be allowed. President Kennedy was already under attack for lowering the required number of U.S. inspections from twenty to seven, while Soviet Premier Nikita S. Khrushchev later indicated he had "gone to the mat" with his Council of Ministers to be able to propose two or three inspections.

Without treaty provisions for on-site inspections, President Kennedy was in a difficult position to secure the consent of two thirds of the Senate necessary to ratify a comprehensive test ban treaty. Seismologists agreed that national technical means might not detect some Soviet underground nuclear tests, and the Joint Chiefs of Staff argued that the Soviet Union could achieve important advances by clandestine tests. The Joint Chiefs were unanimously opposed to a comprehensive test ban agreement, as were important figures in the scientific community and many influential senators.

Given this situation, President Kennedy settled for a limited test ban treaty, in which the risks of undetected Soviet cheating were far less. Even so, a treaty amendment requiring on-site inspections was offered but was defeated by a substantial margin. Most senators accepted the Kennedy Administration's position that on-site inspections were not needed to monitor a limited test ban agreement, and that to make this a condition for ratification would effectively scuttle the treaty. Moreover, the treaty without on-site inspections had the support of the Joint Chiefs, and, as it turned out, all but 19 U.S. senators.

In retrospect, many officials who served in the Kennedy Administration wish that the President had decided to push ahead with a comprehensive test ban. With the passage of time the risks associated with clandestine Soviet underground tests appear less formidable than the advancements in nuclear weapon capabilities that have occurred as a result of underground testing. However, retrospective judgments are of little help to political leaders and elected officials at the time they must make their choices.

The biological weapons convention presents a very different

case study of the scope and verification standards for arms control agreements. In 1972, President Nixon chose the widest possible scope for agreement—a complete ban on the development, production, stockpiling, or acquisition of biological and toxin weapons. Parties to the agreement were allowed, however, to retain undefined types and quantities of biological and toxin stocks for "prophylactic, protective or other peaceful purposes."

The biological weapons convention contained no verification provisions and only the most modest compliance provisions: signatories were to consult and cooperate with one another when problems arose through "appropriate international procedures within the framework of the United Nations." Questions of noncompliance could be pursued by lodging a complaint, including the presentation of evidence, in the UN Security Council. States were to cooperate in carrying out any investigation initiated by the Security Council, which would inform signatories of its findings.

It was widely recognized that these standards for verification and compliance were not rigorous. Nevertheless, the Senate consented to ratification after the most perfunctory debate by a vote of 90–0. Most elected officials agreed with the Nixon Administration's judgment not to pursue intrusive verification procedures. Biological weapons could, after all, be produced in very small facilities. Verification provisions which provided high confidence of treaty compliance would have required the right of entry into large numbers of facilities in the Soviet Union and the United States—something neither side was willing to accept. At the time, the United States had renounced unilaterally an offensive biological weapons capability. For President Nixon, his advisers and most elected officials, strict verification and compliance procedures for the biological weapons convention were less important than having the Kremlin formally subscribe to a position the United States had taken unilaterally.

With the passage of time, many have second-guessed this judgment. Questions of Soviet noncompliance with the convention have been sparked by an outbreak of pulmonary anthrax in Sverdlovsk near a suspected biological weapons facility, and by reports of "yellow rain" in Southeast Asia and Afghanistan. Significantly, this evidence came to light despite the lack of verification provisions in the convention. Compliance questions relating to biochemical warfare highlight the need for satisfactory mechanisms for consultation and investigation of the evidence. They also have convinced most specialists in the field that the standards for verification and compliance established in the convention are unacceptable for future agreements.

The MIRV case study presents a third example of the importance of political decisions relating the scope of an arms control agreement to appropriate standards of verification. During the critical period 1969–71, the Nixon Administration made a calculated decision to continue flight-testing and deployment of MIRVs rather than make serious efforts to limit them in SALT I. Recommendations by some participants to slow down or to halt the MIRV test program while negotiations were under way were rejected by The White House. At the time, the Soviets were constructing 200 new ICBM silos per year and building new missile-carrying submarines at a rate of seven or eight per year. In contrast, U.S. strategic force levels were fairly static; increases in U.S. capabilities rested heavily on the deployment of MIRVs, a program with strong support in the Pentagon and in key congressional offices.

The initial U.S. negotiating position at SALT I was to link a ban on MIRVs to on-site inspections, including inspections of Soviet surface-to-air missile sites as well as the dismantling of large Soviet early-warning radars. According to the prevailing view within the Nixon Administration, MIRVs were needed to counter ABM systems. If MIRVs were to be banned, then intrusive measures were required to provide assurance that Soviet air defenses were not upgraded to provide ABM capabilities. Hence the need for on-site inspections.

The negotiating linkage between a MIRV ban and on-site inspections was unnecessary in a technical sense; it was also unacceptable to the Soviet Union. Bans on the flight-testing of MIRVs and the testing of air defense radars for ABM purposes would have been sufficient to provide assurances against MIRV deployment and air defense upgrades. Indeed, provisions were later worked out for the ABM treaty barring the testing of air defense radars "in an ABM mode," without provisions for on-site inspections. Monitoring a ban on MIRV testing by national technical means was far simpler, since repeated developmental and operational flight tests were required for minimal assurance that warheads could be directed accurately against separate targets. Such flight tests could not be concealed from U.S. intelligence for very long, despite the qualms expressed on this score by some Nixon Administration officials.

For their part, the Soviets were also reluctant to ban MIRVs during SALT I. At the time, the United States had already begun MIRVed developmental flight tests; the Soviets had not. Moreover, at the outset of the SALT negotiations, the Soviet Union was lagging far behind in the number of overall launchers as well as warheads. The Kremlin therefore proposed that MIRV flight-testing be permitted, but deployment prohibited—a proposition that could not be verified with high confidence except by on-site inspection, which, of course, the Soviets adamantly refused to permit.

As SALT I chief negotiator Gerard Smith later recounted, the MIRV proposals tabled by both sides were an ingenious and disingenuous mismatch. It is far from clear whether a MIRV ban could have been negotiated with the Soviet Union during this period, but in retrospect most participants regretted the U.S. decisions to exclude MIRVs from the scope of an agreement and to set such a high standard for MIRV verification. Because MIRVs remained uncontrolled in SALT I, U.S. and Soviet strategic nuclear forces subsequently rose precipitously, impairing the security of both sides.

The lessons to be learned from these case studies depend on subjective evaluations that vary from one analyst to the next. But they all point to the importance of domestic political factors in the choice of an agreement's scope and verification standards. In the limited test ban treaty and MIRV cases, Presidents Kennedy and Nixon chose a course of action that eased political opposition to negotiated agreements, but strong supporters of arms control would argue that short-term political considerations resulted in negative strategic consequences in the long run. On the other hand, Presidents Kennedy and Nixon succeeded in ratifying strategic arms control agreements—even if they were limited in scope.

Future debates over the scope and verification standards for new agreements will come to a head whenever accords governing hard-to-verify weapon systems like mobile missiles and cruise missiles are negotiated. Unlike the nuclear forces included in previous agreements, these weapon systems can be deployed with less-elaborate launch facilities and can be used for a variety of military purposes. For those most concerned about Soviet noncompliance, the more intrusive the U.S. methods of verification for mobile and cruise missiles, the better.

Some people consider on-site inspections necessary for hard-to-verify weapons. On-site inspections can be useful to verify the destruction of stockpiles or to confirm a ban on underground tests, but inspections for mobile and cruise missiles will still be of limited utility while being extraordinarily difficult to negotiate. Neither side is likely to allow unconditional, unlimited on-site inspections and neither is likely to agree to inspections that will provide clear evidence of a violation. Some visits may raise false alarms over cheating when ambiguous evidence turns up. Other inspections may generate a false sense of security indicating compliance at the site visited, but little more. In the final analysis, inspections are no panacea for verification problems. If all goes well, inspections can only provide intelligence analysts with high confidence of compliance at individual sites just prior, during, and immediately after the visit.

Cooperative measures, while not as intrusive as on-site inspections, can be quite helpful in monitoring mobile and cruise missiles. Cooperative measures could provide information about production rates by having sensors at production facilities that could detect the movement of missiles and their transporters from production facilities. Other cooperative measures could include designating the facilities that are used to produce individual types of missiles (and dedicating them entirely to such production), providing data on monthly output, and transferring missiles from production facilities to their next destination by an agreed schedule to facilitate observance by national technical means. Another set of cooperative measures would be required to simplify the process of monitoring missile deployments—such as designating missile deployment areas and prohibiting the existence of such missiles outside these areas.

Counting rules can be applied to provide bookkeeping solutions to near-insoluble monitoring problems associated with weapon systems like cruise missiles. These sorts of counting rules were applied quite successfully to bombers carrying air-launched cruise missiles (ALCMs) in the SALT II treaty: if ALCMs were tested or deployed on a certain type of aircraft, then all aircraft of that type, unless otherwise modified, would fall within agreed ceilings. It is possible to envision another counting rule governing the number of ALCMs per aircraft and the number of aircraft of that type, just as MIRVed capabilities have been assigned to various missile types. These techniques for counting can also be applied to sea-launched cruise missiles (SLCMs) although the results would be even less precise. For example, assumptions could be made concerning how many "weapon stations" are available on ships of a certain class, and how many of these weapon stations would be designated as nuclear-armed cruise missile stations. Assume, for example, that a submarine or surface ship of a certain class has space for 30 weapons of all kinds, including spares. Of these, ten could be designated as nuclear-armed cruise missile stations. If advanced long-range cruise missiles are tested or deployed on a naval platform, then all ships of that class are held accountable within agreed ceilings. Of course, additional cooperative measures would be required to assist each side in monitoring test programs governing SLCMs.

By placing greater reliance on cooperative measures and counting rules, new agreements governing mobile and cruise missiles are still possible, although they will be less precise than previous accords. Nor will such agreements require on-site inspections if their scope is limited to deployed forces, as was the case in SALT I and II.

Those who argue most strongly for on-site inspections also generally favor broadening the scope of future agreements to include missile production and inventory limits. Even with on-site inspections, the United States will have less confidence in its ability to monitor Soviet compliance with agreements limiting missile production and inventories than with agreements like the SALT I and II accords. Moreover, inspections of missile production and storage facilities will be extremely difficult for both sides to accept.

A strong case can be made for limiting the scope of future agreements to deployed forces. At current levels of strategic forces,* production rates and inventory levels are unlikely to have a bearing on the outcome of a nuclear war or on perceptions of the military balance. Agreements that continue to focus on deployed forces would be far easier to negotiate because they would not require on-site inspections.

Critics of new agreements of whatever scope will point to the risks associated with attempts to control hard-to-verify nuclear forces. Supporters will point to the risks of leaving these forces uncontrolled. It takes little skill to postulate verification requirements that are inadequate to the task (as was the case in the biological weapons convention), or that are impossible for the other side to meet (as happened in the MIRV case). No one standard for verification is applicable to all cases, but as a general rule, the conclusion of President Reagan's Commission on Strategic Forces—which employed the services of two former National Security Council advisers, including commission chairman Lt. Gen. Brent Scowcroft (USAF Ret.), four former secretaries of defense, three former CIA directors, and two former secretaries of state—seems worthy of consideration: "The essential test of an effective verification system is that it will detect with a high degree of confidence any set of violations which would have a significant impact on the strategic balance. The commission believes that goal remains within our reach."

3

Soviet Views on Verification

A newspaperman who was stationed in Moscow for several years tells the story about his request to Soviet authorities to visit Murmansk. Yes, he might go, came the reply, but only by train—an arduous journey to this remote northern area. Why, when there are Aeroflot flights to Murmansk? Because foreigners are barred from these flights, which venture near sensitive military areas. Of course, these areas are covered regularly by photoreconnaissance satellites with keener eyesight than even the most enterprising journalist—a fact well known to Soviet authorities. Nevertheless, the travel restriction held.

The Soviet penchant for secrecy is well known and amply documented. Russian secrecy is a protective device with deep cultural, political as well as military roots. As a military asset, secrecy is valued highly. One branch of military science—*maskirovka*—is devoted to the arts of deception and concealment. These practices come naturally to the society that created Potemkin villages, the stage facades used to persuade Empress Catherine the Great of the indigenous development of newly acquired lands. When directed against potential foes, efforts at concealment and deception require far more elaborate plans.

While deeply ingrained, Soviet secrecy is not immutable. Foreign journalists may now fly from Moscow to Murmansk. Similarly, the Kremlin has relaxed somewhat its opposition to measures that make its military capabilities more evident and thus more amenable to arms control agreements. In some respects, the Soviets have had to bow to the inevitable: when they launched Sputnik, the first satellite to orbit the earth, they undermined their case against "open espionage" from overhead. Space satellites could perform the same photoreconnaissance missions as "spy" planes like the U-2. Unlike the U-2, however, earth-orbiting satellites had no choice but to cross national borders. When the Soviets also developed a photoreconnaissance capability from space, they had every reason to acquiesce in such activities.

It took several years for the Soviet position on the peaceful use of space to evolve. Official pronouncements at first noted the "peaceful intent" of Soviet satellites and the "provocative" nature of early U.S. satellite programs, including the Discoverer, America's first photoreconnaissance satellite, launched the same year (1960) a U-2 was shot down over the U.S.S.R. During the Berlin crisis the following year, the Soviet armed forces newspaper, *Red Star*, compared U.S. satellites to U-2 missions: "A spy is a spy, no matter what height it flies."

This Soviet position softened somewhat during the UN deliberations in 1962 on the peaceful uses of outer space. The U.S.S.R. agreed to provide the UN with orbital characteristics of its satellites, but not to identify their functions. The unreservedly hostile Soviet attitude to U.S. satellites also began to change toward the end of 1963. Surely by this time the Kremlin had a working photoreconnaissance capability. In addition, satellites of a different sort allowed both superpowers to monitor the ban on atmospheric tests contained in the limited test ban treaty.

Even after the test ban treaty was signed in 1963, Soviet military writers continued to condemn U.S. espionage from space. It was only in conjunction with the SALT I accords that positive references to national technical means of verification regularly filtered into Soviet commentaries. The role of national technical means was codified in the SALT I agreements which approved of their use "in a manner consistent with generally recognized principles of international law" to verify compliance with the agreements' provisions. In addition, both parties to the SALT I accords agreed not to interfere with national technical means performing these functions, and not to use "deliberate concealment measures" which impeded verification of treaty provisions. The SALT II treaty further elaborated on these principles by including a controversial provision barring the deliberate denial of telemetry whenever this practice impeded verification of treaty provisions. During missile tests, electronic signals—or telemetry—are transmitted from the missile which engineers can then utilize in evaluating the missile's performance. The United States can also utilize these transmissions to make determinations about treaty compliance. Denial could be achieved by several techniques, most notably by encryption*—the transmission of data in code.

The Soviet Union's attitude toward national technical means of verification has evolved, but it still has a way to go. The Kremlin reserves the right to take countermeasures against satellites which are used for "hostile purposes"; Soviet views toward nonsatellite national technical means, such as ground stations used to monitor treaty compliance, remain obscure; and the Kremlin is extremely sensitive about the end use of satellite-derived data for nonmilitary purposes (such as economic forecasting). Soviet maskirovka programs continue unabated, and a crude capability to destroy low-orbiting satellites has been tested.

A further positive change in Soviet attitude toward national technical means appears unlikely at the present time, with negotiations for new arms control agreements stalled, previous agreements unratified, and U.S.-Soviet relations at a low ebb. Indeed, the Kremlin has taken steps to withold the fruits of previous negotiations, as evidenced by compliance controversies over Soviet encryption of telemetry during flight tests of new missiles.

A review of negotiations over nuclear test ban agreements can offer useful insights into Soviet views and negotiating tactics on verification. When these negotiations began in Geneva at The Conference on the Discontinuance of Nuclear Weapon Tests in 1958, the Soviets demanded a veto power in all important decisions, including decisions relating to inspections. The Kremlin initially agreed to the establishment of control posts to monitor a ban on weapon tests within its borders, but the staff of each post as well as the staff director were to be Soviet nationals. A foreigner could serve as "chief control officer," and could accompany carefully circumscribed aircraft inspection flights or ground inspections. Air samplings for radioactivity would be permitted along predetermined routes, and foreign inspectors would be chosen from a registered list of names.

As negotiations proceeded, the Soviets gradually increased the number of foreigners allowed at each control post, but they refused to relinquish their veto power. Otherwise, Soviet Premier Khrushchev asserted, the Kremlin would be handing Soviet "territory over to the supervision of the aggressive NATO (North Atlantic Treaty Organization) bloc." Still later, the Soviet Union proposed an annual quota of on-site inspections not subject to a veto—a maximum of three per year. (The United States demanded a minimum of 20, to go with 21 control posts within the U.S.S.R.) In subsequent negotiations, differences were also narrowed over the number of control posts to be located within the Soviet Union—the Kremlin accepted 15, while the United States lowered its requirement to 19. The Geneva negotiations broke down with the resumption in 1961 of nuclear weapon tests by France, the Soviet Union, and then by the United States, ending a moratorium in effect since 1958.

When negotiations resumed during the Kennedy Administration, the Kremlin at first withdrew its offer of on-site inspections, asserting that all underground tests could be detected by technical means. The Soviet position next reverted to the acceptance of two-to-three on-site inspections, but only three "automatic seismic recovery stations" were deemed acceptable on Soviet soil. The Kremlin declined to talk about the details of inspection procedures until agreement was reached on these numbers. Still later, Premier Khrushchev again withdrew the Soviet offer of on-site inspections, saying that the U.S.S.R. would "never open the doors to NATO spies." The agreement that was finally negotiated in 1963 essentially set aside disputes over the verification for subsequent negotiations, since both sides agreed that a limited test ban treaty could be monitored by national technical means.

A decade of subsequent negotiations produced the Threshold Test Ban Treaty of 1974, which established a 150-kiloton limit on underground tests. In order to verify compliance and to reduce the uncertainty associated with measuring yields of underground tests by national technical means, the Soviets agreed to exchange scientific and technical data, including the geographic coordinates of the boundaries of each test site, information on geological characteristics within them, and geographic coordinates, yields, dates, times and depths of underground weapon tests to be used for calibration purposes. The yields of those tests were to be as near to the 150-kiloton limit as possible.

These provisions have never been put into effect because neither side has ratified the threshold test ban treaty. President Gerald R. Ford deferred ratification, pending completion of a companion agreement governing nuclear explosions for non-military purposes. The Carter Administration deferred ratification, opting instead to negotiate a comprehensive treaty banning all tests. The Reagan Administration has also declined to ratify the threshold test ban treaty, noting the possibility of the Kremlin providing incorrect data, and the lack of treaty provisions allowing for authentication of the data exchanged.

The companion treaty to the threshold test ban treaty, the peaceful nuclear explosion treaty, was signed in 1976 but it, too, has not been ratified. It permitted nuclear explosions for engineering and scientific projects or other peaceful purposes, but with on-site inspections for explosions with aggregate yields over 150 kilotons. For some, the Soviet willingness to allow inspections under these conditions indicated the unlikelihood of higher-yield peaceful nuclear explosions. For others, the Soviets were setting an important precedent for subsequent nuclear arms control negotiations.

The logic of inspections for a peaceful nuclear explosion treaty was hard for the Kremlin to refute, since it is difficult to distinguish peaceful explosions from tests with military applications. The Soviets consistently took the position that requirements for inspections had to be specifically and narrowly related to the tasks of verifying compliance with treaty constraints. The United States sought broader bounds. The American concern about the need for thorough inspections to provide assurance of Soviet compliance was matched by the Soviet concern that inspections would be used as a fishing expedition for espionage purposes. Even relatively simple tasks associated with these inspections, such as the use of cameras, required arduous negotiations. Soviet and U.S. concerns were resolved by providing the U.S.S.R. with access to Western monitoring devices. Two identical sets of equipment would be brought by observers—one to be retained for examination by the host country, the other to be used for measurements. Each set of equipment would contain two recorders, allowing for host and inspectors to each have a copy. The treaty also established a joint consultative commission to discuss any compliance questions that might arise.

Subsequent negotiations for a comprehensive test ban treaty drew on the precedent of inspections established in the peaceful nuclear explosions treaty. Progress was also made in working out the instrumentation to be used by foreign observers, including radiation monitoring devices and seismic recorders, and detailed discussions took place on the installation of unmanned seismic stations within the United States, U.S.S.R. and Britain. The Soviets agreed to accept the placement of tamperproof seismic stations, but differences remained on the number of stations needed. The Kremlin insisted that all three nations accept 10 stations, while the British insisted that a smaller number would suffice for them, since British tests are conducted at the Nevada test site.

As the test ban negotiating history indicates, Soviet flexibility on verification and cooperative measures remains constrained by deep-seated sensitivities about espionage and protection of national security, broadly defined. The Kremlin has been forthcoming in the past on verification questions when there has been a specific reason to do so—such as to secure the benefits of a negotiated agreement—but only to the extent necessary to monitor specific provisions within that agreement. Greater openness is viewed not as an end in itself, but as tied to the object of negotiations. Nor will the Kremlin's negotiators be particularly philanthropic on verification issues. The United States needs intrusive verification provisions far more than does the Soviet Union. Soviet verification proposals invariably are inadequate at the outset of negotiations; they improve over time, but they may also be withdrawn. Attractive verification provisions will usually be offered by the Kremlin in the expectation of gain elsewhere in an agreement; they will be won by the West only in the course of hard bargaining.

As for the future, the Kremlin has indicated its openness to on-site inspections in the comprehensive test ban, chemical weapons and mutual and balanced force reductions (MBFR) negotiations. These agreements would involve tasks—such as checking ambiguous seismic events, destroying chemical munitions, and monitoring the withdrawal of forces through exit/entry points—that usefully can be performed by inspectors on-site.

These are unusual cases, however. Most agreements, in the Soviet view, can be monitored quite adequately by national technical means. This was the Soviet position in the INF and START negotiations before they were suspended as well as with respect to agreements governing antisatellite weapons. In the INF and START talks, the Soviets indicated a willingness to discuss cooperative measures to complement national technical means, but resisted discussions about specific provisions with far more central issues unresolved. The Kremlin has shown little interest to date in intrusive measures to monitor missile production and inventories—limitations of considerable interest to the Reagan Administration in both the INF and START negotiations. Attempts to go well beyond national technical means are usually viewed by the Kremlin either as a means for the United States to gain unwarranted intelligence data or as a smokescreen to mask a disinterest in reaching accords.

4

Treaty Compliance

Domestic debates over treaty compliance, like those over verification, have reflected deep divisions of opinion concerning the Kremlin's objectives and the value of Soviet cheating. In congressional debates, from the limited test ban to SALT II, supporters of arms control argued that Soviet leaders would be unlikely to violate agreements that were in their interest as well as ours; that U.S. capabilities to detect violations of any consequence would further serve as a deterrent; and that if violations took place, the United States could respond appropriately, including, if necessary, abrogation of the agreement in question.

During the limited test ban treaty debate, several potential compliance issues were raised by treaty opponents. Nuclear weapon tests in Lake Baikal in the Soviet Union, in deep space, behind the moon, or under a few feet of earth during periods of heavy cloud cover were deemed possible by those who foresaw a determined Soviet effort to foil U.S. national technical means of verification. The possibility of Soviet nuclear weapon tests at or just over the Chinese border was also raised.

President Kennedy was in a strong position to defuse congressional concerns over Soviet noncompliance. If the Soviets reneged on their treaty commitments in the Kennedy Administration, the

United States could be expected to respond purposefully, as was the case when the Kremlin resumed atmospheric tests in 1961. Moreover, the scenarios that envisaged testing behind the moon or in deep space seemed farfetched, and the presumed value of clandestine cheating quite marginal. A treaty amendment offered by Senator John G. Tower (R-Tex.) calling for on-site inspections was easily defeated, even though the satellites designed to detect atmospheric explosions were anticipated but not yet deployed. Those most opposed to the limited test ban treaty compiled long lists of Soviet violations and broken promises, from the Bolshevik Revolution in 1917 to the Yalta agreement in 1945, but with little effect. The perceived benefits of the treaty clearly seemed worth the risk of Soviet noncompliance.

During the SALT I debate, congressional critics sent mixed messages on prospective compliance problems. Skeptics rallied behind an amendment sponsored by Senator Henry M. Jackson (D-Wash.) requiring future agreements to provide for equal strategic force levels. On the one hand, supporters of the Jackson amendment expressed concern not that the Soviets would cheat, but that they could do great harm without resort to cheating. On the other hand, Senator Jackson and his allies were quite concerned over ambiguities in the agreements, particularly the interim agreement's provisions governing the modernization of ICBM launchers, that could be exploited by the Kremlin.

During the course of the SALT I negotiations, the United States tried to place constraints on new Soviet ICBMs, first by limiting directly missile volume, then by limiting increases in silo dimensions to accommodate new types of missiles. Both sides finally agreed that "in the process of modernization and replacement . . . dimensions of land-based ICBM silo launchers will not be significantly increased." Moreover, they agreed that the term "significantly increased" meant an increase of 10 to 15 percent over existing dimensions of ICBM silos, but the negotiating record did not indicate whether calculations were to be based on existing silo diameter, depth, or both. When calculated on the basis of two dimensions rather than one, the resulting increase in volume could be quite considerable—on the order of 50 percent.

During congressional hearings over the interim agreement, skeptical members of Congress were primarily interested in pinning down favorable interpretations of what would constitute permissible increases in silo volume. There was no shortage of witnesses to endorse the U.S. view that a narrow interpretation limiting increases to one silo dimension, not both, was consistent with the terms of the interim agreement. The Soviet Union did not agree to this unilateral interpretation. The SALT I limits on new ICBM launchers prevented the Kremlin from deploying additional numbers of their heaviest missiles, but did not prevent their lighter missiles from being replaced by far more capable models.

Later, this issue would be a springboard for contentious debates over Soviet SALT violations, but at that time compliance questions did not loom large on the horizon. President Nixon did not need to defend his credentials as a staunch defender of U.S. interests in negotiations with the Soviet Union. Whatever criticism was levied at the SALT I accords was deflected by the President's acceptance of the Jackson amendment and his firm commitment to proceed with the B-1 bomber, Trident submarine and various other programs to strengthen his hand in subsequent negotiations. In addition, the SALT I accords established a special channel, the standing consultative commission,* to handle any compliance questions that might arise.

Concerns over Soviet noncompliance with the SALT I accords contributed to the decision by at least one quarter of the Senate to oppose without reservation the SALT II treaty. As in the past, treaty opponents compiled lists of alleged earlier Soviet transgressions. Unlike Presidents Kennedy and Nixon, President Carter was in a weak position to rebut these charges: the perceived benefits of the SALT II treaty were not greatly appreciated, and the President's resolve in dealing with the Kremlin was widely questioned.

The Standing Consultative Commission

To set the record straight, the Carter Administration released an unclassified report of U.S. and Soviet concerns which had been raised in the standing consultative commission since its inception. The report provided little ammunition either to committed treaty supporters or to critics. Its findings did not dispute those who argued that the Kremlin repeatedly exploited definitional ambiguities and pressed at the margins of the SALT I accords. But the Carter Administration's compliance report did refute assertions of violations, finding that in every instance of troublesome Soviet practices, "the activity has ceased or subsequent information has clarified the situation and allayed our concern."

Presidents Nixon, Ford and Carter studiously avoided an accusatory approach to these compliance issues, seeking instead to fence in problems by working out mutual understandings and common definitions of ambiguous treaty provisions. The clear objective for these Presidents was to maintain the viability of the SALT I accords by halting Soviet practices that could undermine the agreements. Their approach during this period has been described by Robert Buchheim, a former U.S. commissioner at the standing consultative commission, in the following terms:

> The essence of the standing consultative commission implementation task is to head off gross dislocations or irretrievable circumstances by acting early enough and finding mutually acceptable measures to sustain intact the agreements within its field of responsibility.
>
> The initial requirement of this task is to raise potential problems for resolution before they get out of hand and become causes for undesired reconsideration of an entire agreement. Lying in the grass and building a comprehensive case for eventually jumping up and shouting 'gotcha' might be fun for some of the grass-dwellers, but it would not be a sensible way to sustain a desired agreement.

Concerns raised by the United States at the standing consultative commission included the controversy over new types of Soviet missiles, the construction of what initially appeared to be new missile silos despite SALT I's ban on such excavations, Soviet concealment practices associated with new weapon systems, and the possible testing of a surface-to-air missile (SAM) radar in "an ABM mode." Compliance questions raised during this period were resolved in a variety of ways. For example, on the question of new types of Soviet ICBMs that were appreciably larger than their predecessors, the United States did not make headway at the standing consultative commission: despite assertions of violations, the new deployments were not inconsistent with the terms in the interim agreement but with a unilateral U.S. interpretation of the agreement. On the question of excavating new ICBM launchers, the Kremlin's position at the commission was borne out over time: as construction progressed, the United States concluded that these facilities were to control the launch of missiles, not to add to their number. After questions of Soviet concealment practices were raised at the commission in 1974, this pattern of expansion stopped.

The process of clarifying treaty obligations was often an arduous one, as was evident with the compliance problem relating to Soviet radar activity. The ABM treaty obligates both sides not to give missiles, launchers or radars, other than those associated with ABM systems, the capability to counter strategic ballistic missiles or to test them "in an ABM mode." The picture was clouded, however, because there was no agreement on what constituted tests in an ABM mode and because the United States maintained that tests for safety and instrumentation purposes were permitted.

In 1973, U.S. intelligence began to notice Soviet practices that could encroach upon treaty provisions when a radar, eventually identified as one associated with the SA-5 air defense system, had been turned on during the flight-testing of Soviet strategic ballistic missiles. The reason why the radar had been operating was unclear and prompted considerable monitoring by the intelligence community. When, in the Ford Administration, the United States made a rigorous presentation in the standing consultative commission about how SA-5 radar tests could undermine critically important treaty limitations, these tests stopped within three weeks. It then required approximately two years of private diplomacy in the Carter Administration to work out a common agreement governing limits on the operation of air defense radars.

For supporters of the SALT process and the standing consultative commission this case study constituted a success story. For critics, it confirmed how Soviet violations had been swept under the rug by transforming the Kremlin's malpractices into the commission's "solutions." In this view, the Kremlin had unfairly gained military advantages at the expense of negotiated agreements. In contrast, Administration officials during this period took a more relaxed view of Soviet practices, assuming that whatever tests were conducted with a radar associated with the SA-5 system did not provide Soviet air defense crews with much help to counter incoming strategic ballistic missiles. No compensating military initiatives were deemed necessary in response to Soviet crowding at the margins.

To critics of the SALT process, the sluggishness of the U.S. response to compliance problems and to the pace of the Kremlin's strategic modernization programs spelled deep trouble for the immediate future. During the SALT II debate, critics argued that treaty supporters would be loathe to raise allegations of violations, regardless of the evidence. They also argued that the basis for charging the Kremlin with numerous violations was lost due to sloppy negotiating, particularly with respect to limitations on new ICBMs. The Republican party's campaign platform during the 1980 presidential campaign formally pledged to end the "cover-up" of Soviet violations of arms control agreements.

Given key positions of responsibility in The White House, the Pentagon and the Arms Control and Disarmament Agency, critics of compliance diplomacy as practiced under Presidents Nixon, Ford and Carter, pursued very different tactics. They preferred a condemnatory rather than a fact-finding and problem-solving approach in the standing consultative commission. Because they took a more alarmist view of the military implications of Soviet misbehavior, they also believed that patience was not a virtue in dealing with compliance controversies. Nor was fencing in these problems a satisfactory solution: the status quo ante or something close to it was the appropriate answer. It therefore followed that if satisfactory solutions could not be readily achieved in the commission, presidential findings of noncompliance were essential.

Initially, President Reagan declined to endorse the long list of "violations and circumventions" prepared by bitter critics of the SALT I accords but dismissed by his three predecessors. As new compliance issues relating to the unratified SALT II agreement arose, pressures from conservative members of Congress began to mount for a public accounting of Soviet transgressions. As was the case after the interim agreement was signed, the flight-testing of new Soviet ICBMs became a highly contentious issue, fueled this time by earlier assurances from Carter Administration officials that only one new type of Soviet ICBM would be allowed under SALT II. The high level of encryption associated with these missile flight tests appeared inconsistent with the SALT II provision barring such practices when they impeded verification of treaty constraints. The Soviets denied any impropriety, requesting information on data Washington believed was being concealed. Washington rejected this inquiry as a fishing expedition to compromise intelligence sources and methods, a response Moscow no doubt anticipated. Of greater concern was the unexpected construction of a new phased-array radar in Siberia, confirmed in mid-1983. Such radars are versatile enough to be used for a variety of purposes, including ballistic missile defense. The Soviets claim their new radar is for space tracking, a permissible activity under the ABM treaty. However, its siting, orientation and capabilities suggest it is better suited for providing early warning of missile attack, another permissible activity under the treaty, but not at this location.

Protracted debates took place within the Reagan Administration over whether and how SALT II questions should be discussed in the standing consultative commission. Some within the Administration argued against raising SALT II compliance issues since to do so would give the treaty, whose ratification they helped to block, unwarranted standing. At first the U.S. delegation was directed to express concerns about SALT II compliance while refusing to become engaged in a discussion of specific issues. Typically, the commission will meet twice yearly, during the spring and fall. The U.S. delegation began to discuss the issue of new missile types during the spring 1983 session; it raised the

Siberian radar issue in the fall. Other channels also were used to express U.S. concerns. Administration officials were divided over what Soviet actions would constitute a satisfactory response, but they were in accord that the Soviets were unlikely to be forthcoming. At the conclusion of the fall 1983 session, President Reagan issued a report on Soviet noncompliance. Included in the findings were citations of ICBMs that SALT critics had previously considered either unverifiable or within the permissive boundaries of the SALT II treaty.

The public release of the Reagan Administration's findings was immediately questioned by those who felt it lengthened the odds against the commission's being able to resolve issues privately. There was also something incongruous about asserting violations of "political commitments" to agreements that the Administration refused to ratify—as was the case with four of the seven citations in the President's report. The Administration's findings on SALT II noncompliance also seemed premature, given the uncertainties associated with Soviet practices and the possibility of learning more about them, either by national technical means or by waiting for responses to U.S. inquiries made during the fall 1983 session of the commission. While a report to Congress was mandated, the Congress did not set a date for its release, nor did it require findings of noncompliance in highly ambiguous cases.

The tentative language of the Reagan Administration's report on Soviet noncompliance seemed to confirm the wisdom of those who had favored accumulating more evidence before going public with a report. The citations and conclusions in the report varied greatly in degree of importance and in kind, making generalizations difficult. SALT II citations dealt with definitional issues and problems with Soviet concealment practices—the hardy perennials of previous standing consultative commission exchanges. On the troubling yellow rain controversy, important questions remained unanswered even though much data are publicly available. Each of the two principal theories explaining the phenomenon of yellow rain—biochemical warfare by the Soviet Union and its allies or toxin-contaminated bee feces and food—has strengths and weaknesses.

Soviet Missile Test Ranges

Reprinted from *Arms Control Today*, February 1979.

The Reagan Administration's case on yellow rain has been bolstered by the presence of mycotoxins found in environmental and biomedical samples, by refugee, eyewitness and defector reports, and the implausibility of the thesis that honeybees are the source of the problem—or the alternative Soviet thesis that linked yellow rain to the U.S. use of herbicides in Indochina.

The case of those who believe that yellow rain is the result of natural phenomena is bolstered by the presence of pollen in toxin-containing environmental samples, questionable scientific techniques in the government's case, and the absence—with the exception of a single gas mask found in Afghanistan—of munitions or other military equipment associated with mycotoxin use. Perhaps the most difficult and troubling question of all is why the Soviets would choose this form of warfare when other effective military options are available that are not constrained by international agreements.

New evidence providing clearer answers to these questions has virtually dried up since 1982. For some, this confirms Soviet complicity in biochemical warfare and the wisdom of public diplomacy. For others, the absence of recent evidence confirms the shakiness of the Reagan Administration's case and the unscientific standards used to document it at the outset.

Another citation of possible Soviet noncompliance relates to the 150-kiloton testing limit established in the threshold test ban treaty. In this instance, national security officials in the Carter and Reagan Administrations arrived at different conclusions from the same evidence. The Carter Administration concluded that the data on Soviet testing above 150 kilotons were too ambiguous for the United States to assert Soviet violations. In contrast, the Reagan Administration concluded that "while the available evidence is ambiguous, in view of ambiguities in the pattern of Soviet testing and in view of verification uncertainties, and we have been unable to reach a definitive conclusion," the Soviets may have violated the treaty.

The Soviets high-yield weapon tests were held at a site north of the Arctic Circle; lower-yield tests were usually conducted in Kazakhstan, a Soviet Republic adjacent to China and Mongolia.

Experts agree that American seismic readings in the past consistently inflated the yields of Soviet underground tests because of differences in local geology. Experts also agree that the magnitudes of Soviet tests at their Kazakh test site increased from 1977 to 1980. Disagreement begins over the degree to which the United States was overestimating Soviet yields. When this bias was finally adjusted at the outset of the Carter Administration, some felt the recalculations were too modest, others believed them to be too large. Then, when the readings from Soviet underground tests in Kazakhstan subsequently rose, two predictably different explanations were forthcoming. Most of those who felt the bias recalculations excessive believed the Soviets—who were presumably testing at the 150-kiloton limit to begin with—took advantage of the U.S. revisions to test at higher yields, contrary to the threshold test ban treaty. Others felt that the 150-kiloton threshold agreement forced a decision by the Soviets to phase out tests at their remote northern site. They also assumed that tests conducted at the Kazakh site had yields well below 150 kilotons, perhaps because the city of Semipalatinsk is as close to this test area as Las Vegas is to the Nevada test site. According to this theory, the Soviets gradually raised the yields in Kazakhstan to 150 kilotons to gauge the impact of higher-yield testing in Semipalatinsk.

As can be seen from this abbreviated treatment of the yellow rain and threshold test ban controversies, conclusions on Soviet noncompliance can depend as much on basic assumptions as on the evidence at hand. For those who suspect the worst from the Kremlin and from the benefits of Soviet cheating, the evidence is convincing because the Soviets can be expected to cheat. Those who suspect the worst from the Reagan Administration—and who see little or no military value from cheating—will be inclined to dismiss the allegations. Those who resist subjective judgments are left with more questions than answers in dealing with the ambiguities of treaty compliance issues.

5

Compliance Diplomacy

Compliance diplomacy is a natural extension of the negotiating process because no arms control agreement can be written to cover every future contingency. In many instances, agreements will be purposely vague because both sides may not wish to foreclose military options or because they cannot reach a mutually agreeable limitation. It is therefore unreasonable to expect that compliance problems will not arise. But it is also reasonable to expect that agreements will not be undermined at every possible opportunity. In other words, a degree of trust is unavoidable in any negotiating relationship. How treaty signatories interpret their obligations under an agreement and how they respond to compliance questions can spell the difference between erosion and construction of durable arms control agreements. Compliance diplomacy is therefore at least as important and no less difficult than the process of negotiating agreements in the first place. Compliance diplomacy can succeed when treaty signatories exercise care not to undermine previous agreements. It cannot succeed, however, when one or both parties question an agreement's worth or its future viability.

The questioning process begins when treaty signatories take steps that are not expressly prohibited but that undermine agreed limitations. These steps erode the political, if not the military, benefits of arms control agreements. Both the United States and the Soviet Union have hedged their bets in this way, although the Kremlin has been by far the worst offender. The Soviet military places considerable stock in achieving marginal advantages in gray areas, and there are few internal political or bureaucratic checks against their doing so.

The process of mutual hedging is most apparent with respect to the ABM treaty. The ABM treaty prohibits all but modest deployments of defenses against strategic ballistic missiles, but both sides reserved the right to develop defenses against shorter-range tactical ballistic missiles. Technology is blurring this distinction, which the Soviets are exploiting with the development of the SA-X-12 air defense system that may have some capability against the intermediate-range Pershing II missile, now being deployed in Western Europe. Yet if the SA-X-12 can intercept the Pershing II, it might also have some capability against SLBMs, as well. The Kremlin is also encroaching upon the ABM treaty's constraints on new fixed land-based systems by developing rapidly deployable components for such a system. Soviet practices have not as yet created burdensome military problems for the United States, judging by the Defense Department's budget priorities in fiscal year 1985: funds for improved missile penetration capabilities were voluntarily deleted by the Pentagon in an economy move. Nevertheless, military concerns will undoubtedly become greater as the hedging process continues.

The Reagan Administration is also hedging its bets against the demise of the ABM treaty, although U.S. efforts are not nearly so comprehensive or so far along as Soviet activities. Funding has begun to upgrade the Patriot air defense system to produce a tactical ABM capability. The construction of new, large phased-array radars for early warning against missile attacks is also under way in Georgia and Texas. These radars provide coverage for two thirds of the continental United States, notwithstanding a treaty provision requiring radars to be located on a country's periphery, facing outward. They complement coverage now provided by radars constructed previously on the east and west coasts and at Grand Forks, North Dakota. None of these radars is inferior to the large Soviet phased arrays which ABM treaty critics insist have an ABM "battle management" capability.

Current ABM developments are the clearest example of how military programs, however they are characterized, can raise questions about each side's intentions and lead to the unraveling of negotiated agreements. At some point, existing agreements can erode to the extent that they cease to be in the national security interest of the disadvantaged side. Well before this point is reached, however, serious political problems may jeopardize the treaty regime. Americans in increasing numbers are beginning to ask whether it is possible to do business with a negotiating partner who regularly acts in ways that undermine solemn political compacts. For example, Soviet concealment practices may well be deeply rooted in the Russian psyche but they also raise compliance problems while generating broader concerns over Soviet intentions. Moreover, the Kremlin consistently authorizes new missile programs that provide only marginal improvements over their predecessors but produce major compliance headaches.

A parallel reevaluation must also be well under way in the Kremlin. While U.S. critics of arms control believe the Kremlin has achieved substantial gains as a result of the SALT process, it is doubtful the Soviet leadership takes a similar view. True, strategic arms control negotiations have legitimized the Kremlin's standing as a coequal to the United States, but in the Soviet view, they have not produced many concrete benefits nor are they likely to do so in the near future. No offensive U.S. nuclear weapon program has been blocked as a result of negotiated agreements, while U.S. strategic offensive capabilities have climbed at a steady rate. In the "decade of neglect" so often mentioned by Reagan Administration officials, the United States spent approximately $1 trillion for national defense; the number of warheads carried by U.S. strategic forces doubled; the number of sea-based warheads grew fivefold. The Kremlin leadership must share the blame for its deteriorating security position: Soviet strategic programs, which proceeded at a faster pace than U.S. efforts during the decade of the 1970s, have generated a vigorous U.S. response. But the Kremlin cannot be blamed for the vicissitudes of American politics that have contributed to the lack of progress in strategic arms control. U.S. negotiating positions and objectives have changed markedly from one President to the next, and even within the same Administration. Since 1972, no American President has managed to secure ratification of a strategic arms control agreement.

The standing consultative commission succeeded in ironing out compliance questions during the Nixon, Ford and Carter Administrations because neither side questioned the other's basic intentions toward the SALT agreements. Successes were possible despite the ups and downs of superpower relations because both nations had shared perceptions of the benefits of the SALT accords and the risks of their unraveling. In both capitals, these calculations have changed dramatically over the last three years. Hedges, past and prospective, are accumulating to the point where both sides are questioning each other's intentions toward previous agreements as well as the value of the negotiating relationship.

Reagan Administration officials have long held the view that the Soviets would abide by the SALT accords only until they could gain more by breaking out of treaty restraints. Numerous public statements by these officials must have heightened similar Soviet concerns about U.S. intentions. Former Secretary of State Alexander M. Haig Jr. declared to the Senate Foreign Relations Committee that SALT II was "dead"; Secretary of Defense Caspar W. Weinberger announced that U.S. defense programs were in conformity with SALT I and II restraints as a matter of coincidence rather than design, and the President's White House counselor, Edwin Meese III, stated that the Reagan Administration had no moral or legal commitment to abide by expired or unratified SALT agreements. Secretary of State George P. Shultz expressed similar reservations about extending SALT II limitations beyond their expiration date in 1985.

Moreover, several military programs championed by the Reagan Administration telegraphed a lack of interest in maintaining SALT limitations. The Carter Administration's plans for deploying the MX missile were scrapped in favor of "dense-pack"—a scheme that would have required digging holes for new missiles, an activity prohibited by the SALT I interim agreement and the SALT II treaty. Administration officials explained that the excavations would be allowed because they were for new "hardened capsules" rather than silos, and would be completed after the expiration of SALT II, in any event. Later, the President agreed to press ahead with a second new ICBM—the Midgetman—to complement the MX. Again, its deployment would be allowed because it would take place after the terms of the SALT II agreement, which permitted only one new type of ICBM, had expired. Then the President endorsed a "star wars" defense against nuclear attack, a goal that was utterly at odds with the ABM treaty. Ongoing ABM research projects, such as the Talon Gold program to test a laser's ability to acquire and track targets in space, also would pose treaty compliance problems. Like the MX, the Talon Gold program predated the Reagan Administration, but it must have had a less ominous character to the Soviets under the auspices of an Administration committed to the SALT agreements and uncommitted to star wars. In this context, the Reagan Administration's handling of compliance issues—its public diplomacy, initial refusals to engage in standing consultative commission discussions and then issuance of a report on noncompliance—must have fueled Soviet suspicions about the Administration's future commitment to SALT limitations.

As the unraveling process becomes increasingly apparent, it also becomes increasingly difficult to stop. Both sides seek to protect themselves against worst-case scenarios by defining treaty obligations in still more-permissive ways or by exploiting ambiguities in treaty texts. Neither side is going to be left at the starting gate when its negotiating partner pulls out of the agreements. The process of encroachment on agreed limitations is not as blatant as ardent SALT critics—no doubt in the Soviet Union as well as in the United States—contend, but its damaging cumulative political impact is undeniable. Compliance problems feed on themselves when treaty signatories question each other's long-term objectives. Political relations continue to sour and the checks against this unraveling process are weakened. In the current environment, imagine a meeting of political and military officials in the United States and the U.S.S.R.: who would argue not to hedge bets against current arms control agreements for fear of undermining them further?

It is natural for great powers to slough off restraints on their armaments when they are increasingly suspicious of their adversaries' intentions. Nevertheless, U.S. and Soviet leaders have good reason to avoid a nuclear arms competition free from even the modest constraints imposed by the SALT agreements. When the atomic and hydrogen bombs were developed, who could have predicted that nuclear forces would have reached current levels, or that requirements for improved capabilities would still be so pressing? In the absence of SALT controls, U.S. and Soviet military requirements will grow far greater still. Despite their misgivings, both nations will be driven into this accelerated competition because neither side can afford not to compete; to fall behind in the competition confers too many political, if not military, disadvantages. To avoid these pitfalls, the object of U.S. and Soviet diplomacy should be to shore up arms control agreements reached during the SALT decade.

Breaking the Deadlock

In theory, a President with Ronald Reagan's hardline, anti-Communist credentials has more leeway to brake this process of decontrol than Presidents of a more liberal bent. Likewise, conservative Presidents are better able to defuse concerns over treaty verification and compliance by appealing for public trust in their judgment that the United States can monitor Soviet compliance and respond effectively to Soviet misbehavior. By large majorities, the electorate and the Congress also would be inclined to trust Reagan's judgment that previous compliance problems should not stand in the way of new agreements. Irreconcilables in the Congress would bitterly contest these findings, but they can be isolated effectively with an erstwhile ally in The White House.

Ever since Reagan was elected, this scenario has sustained those who want the President's pragmatism to prevail over his ideology. After all, ideologues in the Kremlin have long since demonstrated an ability to deal with hardliners in The White House when it was in their interest to do so. Reagan, however, has not been an activist President with respect to negotiations, and no nuclear arms control agreement has ever been reached without the active intervention of a sitting President. He has yet to demonstrate a substantive grasp of the issues under negotiation, or a sense of priorities and trade-offs needed to achieve them. Nor does he have a strong and experienced figure to assist him in either the Cabinet or The White House. These deficiencies have been blurred by the absence of effective leadership in Moscow and the rigidity of Soviet negotiating positions. Even with key changes in personnel in the Reagan Administration, the possibility of progress in negotiations is uncertain. But without such changes, it is difficult to see how President Reagan can make headway in arms control negotiations or in compliance diplomacy.

Any President to the left of Reagan faces an entirely different set of problems on verification and compliance issues. The more such a President is inclined to take risks for arms control benefits, the more vulnerable he will be in the domestic political arena, particularly if he is perceived as lax in pursuing strategic modernization programs or unsteady in his handling of U.S.-Soviet relations.

Arms control-oriented Presidents will be especially sensitive to news leaks of compliance problems, immediately characterized as violations by those opposed to arms control agreements. There are no easy remedies to prevent compliance issues from cropping up or to resolve them after they arise. Improved national technical means of verification may encourage American Presidents to enter into agreements they might otherwise avoid, and generate support for those agreements by wider segments of the Congress and the public. But better monitoring capabilities may also generate a greater number of false alarms bearing on compliance. Nor do improved national technical means prevent problems from arising when signatories define their treaty obligations in unhelpful ways. Detecting such troubling activities has not been the problem in the past; the problem lies in defining an appropriate response.

Concerns over Soviet compliance can also be alleviated somewhat by avoiding difficult-to-verify provisions. The SALT II provision governing modifications in ICBMs is a case in point. In order to allow some latitude for U.S. military planners, the Carter Administration settled on provisions permitting 5 percent leeway on certain ICBM parameters to distinguish between acceptable modifications of existing missiles and limitations on "new" missile types. This was certainly better than allowing 25 percent improvements, but the SALT II new-types provision proved exceedingly costly. It was difficult to negotiate, difficult to defend during ratification hearings, and politically damaging when Soviet missile designers and political leaders took up the challenge of shoehorning new missiles into the 5 percent rule. In addition, the new-types provision required Soviet cooperation on encryption, which was easily withheld when the United States declined to ratify the treaty.

Future Presidents would be wise to avoid these political minefields and seek alternative ways to reduce the military potential of Soviet ICBMs. Should the object of U.S. compliance diplomacy be to prevent the Soviet Union from spending billions of rubles for marginal improvements in ICBM capabilities? The number of new types of ICBMs either side deploys is less important than reducing their number of deployed warheads, tied to counting rules and constraints on ICBMs that can carry multiple warheads.

More-intrusive verification provisions, as with improvements in national technical means, may not necessarily help in treaty compliance questions. As discussed earlier, on-site inspection can be a useful tool at times, but it is hardly a cure-all for treaty compliance. Precise treaty language can also promote treaty compliance, but as previous negotiators have discovered, precise formulations are not always easy to arrive at. In the past, those most concerned about verification and compliance have called for precision in agreements reached. Now many of these voices call for simplicity. It is difficult, however, to see how simple agreements, if we were willing and able to negotiate them, could relieve the United States of compliance questions when detailed provisions have failed to do so in the past.

In the current political environment, compliance diplomacy cannot be effective unless and until both sides clarify their intentions toward existing nuclear arms control agreements. The unratified SALT II limitations expire at the end of 1985; the SALT I interim agreement's provisions expired in October 1977. The Reagan Administration has stated its willingness not to undercut the limitations of the interim agreement and the SALT II treaty, provided the Soviet Union shows similar restraint. Soviet spokesmen have made similar conditional statements. With strained U.S.-Soviet relations and with compliance problems mounting, there is a growing prospect that limits on offensive forces will fall by the wayside. At this point, the most effective signal U.S. and Soviet leaders could make to indicate their commitment to continued SALT compliance would be to announce the extension of SALT I and II ceilings on offensive forces. An American initiative to proceed with ratification of the threshold test ban treaty and peaceful nuclear explosions treaty would also signal U.S. intent to affirm treaties negotiated during the SALT decade. The Reagan Administration has repeatedly expressed reservations about these steps, but none would harm U.S. security or alter current U.S. practices.

Official intentions toward the ABM treaty present a more difficult problem, given the scope of current Soviet activities and President Reagan's star-wars initiative. But Soviet activities do not begin to provide the Kremlin with an effective capability to defend the U.S.S.R. against nuclear attack. Likewise, star-wars research activities are a long-term proposition that will proceed in the face of daunting technical challenges and limited resources. Both sides are well aware of these constraints—constraints that provide a strong military rationale for maintaining the ABM treaty in place. Nevertheless, tests in space of new technologies with military applications will continue in both countries, even if President Reagan's objective of a futuristic defense is abandoned by his successors. The standing consultative commission will have the difficult task of reaching common agreements on how these tests can be squared with ABM treaty obligations.

Other actions can be taken by both Washington and Moscow to restore confidence in the negotiating process. Confidence is undermined when both sides engage in public diplomacy and table one-sided negotiating positions. The U.S. Congress must play a more constructive role in future debates, recognizing the risks of torpedoing new agreements. We must avoid unrealistic and unnecessary verification requirements which foreclose opportunities for new agreements and raise Soviet questions about U.S. intentions.

For its part, the Soviet Union must be far more sensitive toward treaty constraints than it has been in the past. Parties to an agreement have a right to expect that negotiated agreements will not be consistently undermined by actions not expressly prohibited. The Kremlin must have strong leadership willing and able to say "no" to powerful interest groups that are skeptical of U.S. intentions and eager to exploit ambiguities in treaty texts. The Soviet Union must also be far more forthcoming in meeting U.S. concerns about verification. After all, cooperative measures that improve confidence in treaty compliance do not pose a threat to Soviet security and will be necessary if hard-to-verify systems are to be included in future agreements.

If U.S. and Soviet leaders are able to assuage concerns over each other's intentions toward the SALT accords, it will again be possible to iron out compliance problems in the standing consultative commission. To succeed in this task, and to regain the public's confidence in compliance diplomacy, an Administration must lay out a positive strategy for dealing with compliance issues, indicating the steps it plans to take when questions arise. As a result of previous controversies, it is no longer sufficient for a President, regardless of his political orientation, to say these allegations have no merit or that they are being addressed in quiet diplomatic exchanges.

With the downturn in U.S.-Soviet relations and increased concerns over treaty compliance, it would be wise for American

Presidents to adopt an explicit two-track strategy on compliance questions: the United States should first try to achieve a satisfactory explanation of or solution to compliance concerns through diplomatic channels, moving to countermeasures if diplomatic channels fail. For SALT-related issues, the diplomatic track should start with the standing consultative commission, where there are procedures and precedents to iron out compliance problems in mutually acceptable ways. Other diplomatic channels should be used sparingly, since the commission is best suited to resolve problems that arise. Nevertheless, it may be necessary to reinforce or facilitate the work of the commission by higher-level diplomatic exchanges. As a general rule, it makes little sense to issue public reports or presidential findings of noncompliance while the diplomatic track is being used, since "going public" will only make satisfactory solutions in private harder to achieve.

If compliance diplomacy does not yield a satisfactory solution, offsetting actions may be required. If this second track is needed, countermeasures should be proportional to Soviet activities, since overreactions would only further undermine negotiated agreements. It would be unwise to assume further undetected violations unless and until the intelligence community can document them. Countermeasures should also be within treaty constraints whenever possible, since their purpose is to convey U.S. willingness to maintain the viability of current agreements and its determination to take effective action when the viability of an arms control agreement is challenged. A positive two-track compliance strategy will place U.S. Presidents in a better position to respond to the substantive and political problems arising from Soviet compliance questions. The details for implementing such a strategy cannot be spelled out in advance, since specific responses will depend on individual cases and since Presidents must have flexibility to handle compliance problems when they arise.

Military countermeasures in response to evidence of noncompliance may be appropriate in some instances but not wise or appropriate in others. For example, the Reagan Administration has not proposed that the United States should resume development and production of biological warfare agents as a result of evidence that the Soviet Union has not lived up to its obligations under the biological weapons convention and the 1925 Geneva protocol. A conclusive explanation for yellow rain may never be available. In the event of new reports, the most appropriate response may again be public presentation of the evidence, since private attempts to stop these practices or to elicit explanations for them have not been successful in the past. Early resort to public diplomacy makes sense when there are reports of casualties, when private bilateral exchanges are unsatisfactory, and when the arms control agreements governing these practices have no consultative or compliance provisions.

For nuclear arms control compliance questions, public diplomacy should be the course of last resort, unless the activity in question poses serious security problems that mandate quick action. Diplomatic channels tend to work slowly, especially when complex treaty provisions and military practices are involved. No substantive issue has ever been resolved quickly in the standing consultative commission. Still, the time consumed in the commission will be only a small fraction of that involved in deploying new nuclear weapon systems.

If, after the course of extended efforts by the commission, the United States receives no satisfactory explanation for Soviet activities, public reports explaining U.S. diplomatic efforts, Soviet responses, and the rationale behind U.S. countermeasures are essential. In the current controversy over the new Soviet radar in Siberia, the most sensible course of action is to reach a common understanding in the commission limiting the number of large phased-array radars, regardless of their stated purpose. If the United States cannot achieve this result in the commission and if the Kremlin continues deployment, the President could build additional U.S. radars and/or improve the penetration capability of U.S. offensive nuclear forces. The choice of countermeasures requires considerable skill since what appears proportional to one side may appear disproportionate to the other. The countermeasures must also be chosen wisely to secure congressional and public support, and to elicit an appropriate response from the Kremlin. On the latter point, the Kremlin's reading of an Administration's intentions is critical, as is the political context in which countermeasures are adopted.

In the above-mentioned case, the most appropriate U.S. response would be to improve the penetration capabilities of U.S. offensive nuclear forces. The intent of the U.S. signal should be to uphold the viability of the ABM treaty, not to accelerate its demise. A President committed to the ABM treaty is in the best position to convey this signal. He also has the option of deploying defensive countermeasures without necessarily implying a lack of commitment to the treaty. The same action chosen by an Administration deeply skeptical of the ABM treaty would likely convey the entirely different message of preparing to withdraw from treaty constraints.

Compliance problems undermine the possibility of new agreements as well as those already in force. In a different political environment, Moscow might see the wisdom of establishing consultative bodies to handle compliance questions for those agreements that now lack them. In addition, future Presidents may find it necessary to endorse safeguards against prospective compliance problems. Like the use of proportional countermeasures in ongoing disputes, the purposes of safeguards are twofold: to encourage strict Soviet compliance and to assure the American public that U.S. interests will be protected in the event of troubling Soviet behavior.

The concept of safeguards is not new. President Kennedy committed himself to a program of underground tests and President Nixon supported several strategic modernization programs in order to secure congressional approval of the limited test ban treaty and SALT I accords, respectively. In retrospect, many have expressed misgivings over these trade-offs, suggesting it would have been wiser to initiate this process early in negotiations rather than after their conclusion. Establishing criteria for safeguards early on can help minimize the substantive and political risks of entering into an agreement. For example, an antisatellite agreement clearly poses risks if the Kremlin fails to comply, although these risks seem less injurious to U.S. security than the risks of an unfettered competition in antisatellite warfare. If the Soviets cheat on an antisatellite test ban, there are several alternative safeguards to assure a timely and appropriate U.S. response, including the establishment of an antisatellite weapon production line which can be started if the Soviets resume antisatellite tests.

As in the case of proportional countermeasures, there is no substitute for choosing reasonable safeguards. If an Administration believes the risks of entering into an antisatellite or any other arms control agreement are inordinately large, the preferred safeguards are likely to be so excessive as to foreclose the possibilities of an accord or to minimize its value. An arms-control-oriented President is not likely to share this calculus of benefits and risks; his selection of prudent safeguards can encourage strict Soviet compliance and make a difference in the outcome of ratification debates.

It should be evident from this discussion that compliance diplomacy is at least as difficult and critical as the process of negotiating arms control agreements with the Soviet Union. To be successful at both, future Presidents will need considerable skill along with much imagination and common sense. These traits may still not be sufficient for Presidents of a moderate-to-liberal bent. They can propose well-reasoned and artful strategies to deal with verification and compliance problems and still not be in a position to convince skeptics. Arms-control-oriented Presidents must assume the unalterable opposition from ideologues on the right; their success will depend on convincing the political center that the benefits of agreements negotiated under their auspices are worth the attendant risks. Presidents with reputations for vacillation or weakness are unlikely to succeed in convincing the electorate to take these risks, particularly during periods of disturbing Soviet activities in areas unrelated to arms control agreements.

The Senate is not as hostile to arms control as it was during the SALT II debate. Events in the interim have led to second thoughts, with more senators inclined to play constructive, supportive roles. Nevertheless, approximately one fifth of the Senate is likely to oppose future agreements executed by anyone but a conservative President—the same proportion of senators who opposed the limited test ban treaty in 1963.

Unlike conservative Presidents, moderates cannot expect to sway these votes; it would be a mistake for them to try to do so, both at the outset of negotiations or after their conclusion. The most effective way to outweigh concerns over verification and compliance is to bring home agreements that will generate widespread and enthusiastic public support. If the benefits of agreements are strongly appreciated, verification and compliance risks will not weigh heavily in public debate, as was the case during the limited test ban treaty. If public support is not forthcoming, these issues will resonate strongly, as was the case during the SALT II debate. Future agreements do not need to yield immediate, significant results to meet this criterion, but they must promise steady, progressive benefits over time. Otherwise, future Presidents most inclined to reach arms control agreements with the Kremlin may find themselves unable to secure the necessary votes for them.

In the current political environment, new agreements are unlikely to be negotiated; U.S. and Soviet leaders will be hard pressed simply to maintain agreed limitations that are only tentatively in place. Although it makes emminently good sense to honor these limitations on nuclear forces, the political dynamics of the current impasse are leading both superpowers to continue to hedge their bets. These hedges will increase the strategic capabilities of both sides while confirming bleak assessments of each other's intentions. At a time when strong political leadership is desperately needed, neither Washington or Moscow appears able to halt the slide towards decontrol.

GLOSSARY

Terms in the text followed by an asterisk are defined here.

ABM (antiballistic missile): A defense system which detects incoming missiles and then attempts to track, target and destroy them using radars and interceptor missiles.

antisatellite: A weapon system that tracks, intercepts and destroys orbiting satellites.

counting rules: Rules designed to simplify verification of numerical limits set by negotiated agreements.

encryption: The transmission of electronic signals, such as those from weapon systems under test, in code to conceal information.

geosynchronous: Relating to an artificial satellite that travels above the equator and at the same speed as the earth rotates.

INF (intermediate-range nuclear forces): Forces composed of nuclear-armed missiles and bombers with ranges over 1,000 km. but below the 5,500 km. benchmark used to define an intercontinental ballistic missile (ICBM) in the SALT II agreement. Forces include the U.S. Pershing IIs and ground-launched cruise missiles and the Soviet SS-20 missiles.

interim agreement: See SALT I.

limited test ban treaty: Signed by the United States, Soviet Union and Britain in 1963, the treaty prohibits the testing of nuclear weapons in the atmosphere, in outer space or underwater but permits unlimited testing underground.

MIRV (multiple independently targetable reentry vehicle): The packaging of more than one nuclear warhead atop a single ballistic missile. Each warhead can be directed to a separate target.

national technical means (of verification): Devices under national control used to monitor other countries' military activities as well as their compliance with arms control agreements. National technical means can include photoreconnaissance satellites and radars based on land, sea and in space.

payload: The carrying capacity of any aircraft or missile system. Payload may be used for bombs or missile warheads, guidance equipment and/or penetration aids.

phased-array radar: An advanced radar that scans electronically for objects traveling through space. Phased-array radars can be used for national technical means, early warning of an attack, or for ABM systems.

photoreconnaissance satellites: Satellites capable of taking high-resolution photographs in space.

SALT I and II (strategic arms limitation talks): A series of negotiations between the United States and the Soviet Union that began in November 1969. In May 1972, two agreements were signed. The ABM treaty, of unlimited duration, limited ABM systems; the interim agreement, of five-years' duration, limited ICBM and submarine-launched ballistic missile (SLBM) launchers. Subsequent negotiations produced the SALT II treaty in 1979. The agreement set limits on ICBM and SLBM launchers and on intercontinental-range bombers, as well as various sublimits, including a limit on multiple warhead launchers. SALT II was not ratified by either nation but both the United States and U.S.S.R. agreed not to undercut its provisions.

standing consultative commission: A U.S.-Soviet body established to implement the SALT I and II accords and to consider problems relating to compliance.

START (strategic arms reduction talks): The START negotiations, which followed the SALT talks, began in June 1982 and were suspended in December 1983.

strategic forces: Weapons of intercontinental range included in the SALT accords. They could destroy an enemy's war-making capacity and society. The Soviet Union considers any nuclear weapon that could land on its territory a "strategic" weapon.

telemetry: Data electronically transmitted from a weapon system during testing. The data reveals much about the weapon's performance and characteristics.

throw-weight: Comparable to payload; the combined weight of all warheads, guidance systems and penetration aids carried by a missile. Throw-weight is one measure of the military potential of strategic forces.

Talking It Over
A Note for Students and Discussion Groups

This issue of the HEADLINE SERIES, like its predecessors, is published for every serious reader, specialized or not, who takes an interest in the subject. Many of our readers will be in classrooms, seminars or community discussion groups. Particularly with them in mind, we present below some discussion questions—suggested as a starting point only—and references for further reading.

Discussion Questions

What role do subjective judgments play in determining whether or not the Soviets are complying with negotiated agreements?

Do you agree with the author's assessment of why compliance problems have become more serious? If not, what do you think are the reasons for current compliance controversies? What do you think the United States should do about them?

The author asserts that the risks of noncompliance must be weighed against the benefits of arms control agreements. How can risks be minimized most effectively? Are there agreements that provide significant benefits without significant risks? What kinds of agreements offer the greatest benefits at least risk?

Do you think the United States should seek to control hard-to-verify weapons like mobile and cruise missiles? What standards of verification should be applied to them? Do you agree with the author's assertion that future agreements should be limited to deployed forces, or should they also include production and inventory limits?

Do you think it will be possible for the United States and U.S.S.R. to reach new arms control agreements, given current problems of verification and compliance?

READING LIST

Buchheim, Robert W., and Caldwell, Dan, "The US-USSR Standing Consultative Commission: Description and Appraisal." Working Paper #2. Center for Foreign Policy Development, Brown University, Providence, R.I., May 1983.

Carnegie Endowment for International Peace, "Challenges for U.S. National Security." Final Report. CEIP, 11 Dupont Circle, N.W., Washington, D.C., 20036, 1983. Includes chapters on "The Soviet Approach to Arms Control" and "Verification."

Einhorn, Robert J., "Treaty Compliance." *Foreign Policy* No. 45, Winter 1981-82. Suggestions for compliance diplomacy.

Gray, Colin, "Moscow Is Cheating." *Foreign Policy* No. 56, Fall 1984. A critique of Soviet compliance and recommendations for action.

Meyer, Stephen, "Verification and Risk in Arms Control." *International Security*, Spring 1984. A discussion of uncertainty and risk in verifying compliance with negotiated agreements.

Potter, William C., *Verification and SALT: The Challenge of Strategic Deception*. Boulder, Colo., Westview Press, 1980. Essays keyed to the SALT II agreement from supporters and skeptics.

President's Report to the Congress on Soviet Noncompliance with Arms Control Agreements. The White House, Office of the Press Secretary, Jan. 23, 1984.

Sloan, Stanley R., and Gray, Robert C., "Nuclear Strategy and Arms Control: Challenges for U.S. Policy." HEADLINE SERIES 261. New York, Foreign Policy Association, Nov./Dec. 1982.

Stoertz, Howard, Jr., "Monitoring a Nuclear Freeze." *International Security*, Spring 1984. Considerations involved in monitoring a freeze agreement like that passed by the House in 1983.

U.S. Department of State, "SALT One: Compliance. SALT Two: Verification." Selected Document No. 7. Washington, D.C., Bureau of Public Affairs, U.S. Department of State, Feb. 1978.

"The United States Violates its International Commitments." *News and Views from the U.S.S.R.* Soviet Embassy, Information Department, Washington, D.C., Jan. 30, 1984. The Soviet response to the Reagan Administration's noncompliance report.